# OCCUPIED!

GW00567452

Discover life in the
Bailiwick of Guernsey
under German Occupation

Written and Illustrated by

## VICTORIA ROBINSON

BLUE
ORMER

Published by Blue Ormer Publishing, 2020.
www.blueormer.co.uk

Text and illustrations, copyright © 2020 Victoria Robinson.

ISBN 978-1-9993415-5-8

Printed by Colour Monster, Guernsey.

# CONTENTS

# LIFE BEFORE OCCUPATION

**The Bailiwick of Guernsey lies in the English Channel between England and France. It is made up of Alderney, Sark and Herm, two smaller islands, Brecqhou and Jethou and of course, Guernsey itself. The Channel Islands are called Crown Dependencies and have their own government but rely on the United Kingdom for defence and other matters.**

In 1939, the Second World War began. On the 1st September, Germany invaded Poland. France and England had both agreed to protect Poland if Germany invaded and so when it did, they declared war. Germany and its allies, including Italy and Japan, were known as the Axis powers. They were fighting against the Allied powers which included Britain, France and later on, the USA and Russia.

Germany was led by Adolf Hitler who was Führer – the German leader. He was also head of the Nazi Party – a political organisation which had extreme views. Hitler came to power in 1933 and gained more and more power, forming a regime known as the Third Reich. During the late 1930s, he had begun to seize other countries such as Austria and Czechoslovakia.

Before the war began, the Guernsey people went about their days with few worries and the community lived together happily. The main industries on the island were growing and quarrying. Large areas of the island were covered by greenhouses growing tomatoes. Many people were employed picking and packing tomatoes which were shipped to England. Guernsey Toms were well known throughout the UK. Guernsey granite was another major export. It was extracted from quarries, mainly in the north of the island, and, each year, thousands of tonnes were shipped to the mainland where it was used to construct roads and buildings. Life in Guernsey was busy but happy and peaceful. But all of this soon changed.

*Many homes had greenhouses attached to them or on their land where the local people would grow tomatoes.*

# THE GERMANS ARE COMING

**Once the war began some of the local people signed up and left to join the armed forces. For a few months, the conflict didn't have much of an effect on the Channel Islands, however, this did not last for long.**

By early 1940, Hitler's forces were rapidly moving through Europe, gaining control of more and more land, eventually reaching France. On the 14th June 1940, Paris, the French capital, fell to German control. Within days they were reaching the French coast in Normandy, just a few miles from the Channel Islands. Looking out towards France behind Herm and Jethou, it seemed possible that enemy ships could appear on the horizon at any moment.

Guernsey's spring of 1940 had arrived in a blaze of glorious sunshine but along with the sunny days came the rumours. Lots of people began to think it was likely that the Germans would soon invade and as time went by they realised it was almost certainly going to happen. The locals had to get ready for the war to arrive at their doorstep and it was a worrying time.

*Guernsey people would look out for any signs of the Germans invading from the French coast.*

# TO STAY OR TO GO?

**Plans were put in place to prepare for the impending German invasion. On the 19th June, the newspapers published the headline that there was to be an evacuation of school-age children and mothers with younger children. It also reported that the Channel Islands were going to be demilitarised meaning they would no longer be defended by the British forces.**

The British government knew this was a big risk but decided they could not protect them. They were small and not of strategic importance, meaning that losing them to the Germans would not have had much effect on the overall war effort. The British troops stationed in the islands left immediately as they were needed more urgently elsewhere in Europe. The Royal Court ordered that the Guernsey Militia should be disbanded, any defence uniforms or firearms should be handed in and men of military age were encouraged to leave the island too. Guernsey was in grave danger of being occupied and now there would be no one left to defend it.

The prospect of the Germans invading was terrifying and many people wanted to evacuate to England. To begin with, the main priority was getting as many children as possible to safety. A limited number of boats were available meaning that, at first, other islanders were not allowed to leave until the children had left.

At 4 o'clock in the afternoon on the 19th June, the headteachers of all the islands' schools summoned their pupils' parents and explained the arrangements. Evacuations were to start the next day. The parents had just hours to decide whether to send their children and to pack and prepare everything they needed for their journey to England. These few hours were a heart-breaking time for families. They had to make terribly difficult decisions of whether or not to let their children evacuate, not knowing when they would see them again, or to let them stay at home and face the dangers of occupied rule.

The next day on the morning of the 20th June, large numbers of children and teachers were assembled ready to catch the boat. In a few days around 5,000 school children had evacuated the island. Once they had arrived in England they were taken to Lancashire, Yorkshire, Cheshire and Scotland by train and from there to centres where families in the area would take them in and offer them accommodation and care.

Eventually around 20,000 of Guernsey's population of 44,000 people left before the Germans arrived. The remaining islanders had to adjust to so many people leaving in just a few days and the sadness of separation from friends and family. Evacuations affected most areas of island life. Some businesses closed down and many people no longer had jobs as their employers had gone. Life had changed significantly and things could not have seemed much worse. That was until a terrifying event occurred a few days later.

**WHAT DO YOU THINK...**

it would have been like to know you were leaving Guernsey in only a few hours?

What would you have chosen to take with you?

*The newspapers printed the announcement of evacuations and the instructions for leaving.*

# THE ISLAND UNDER ATTACK

**On the 27th June, planes from the German air force, the Luftwaffe, flew over the island to investigate what was going on from the air. The next day they came back to find out more information.**

As they flew over the harbour they saw a line of lorries waiting to load their cargo onto boats. These were packed with tomatoes waiting to ship the crops to England but from above they looked like military lorries. By mistake, the Germans had not been told that the island was demilitarised and assumed the vehicles were full of supplies needed to defend Guernsey. They bombed the harbour, destroying the lorries and several buildings and scattered the town area with machine-gun fire. It was an awful attack and 34 people were killed with many more badly injured.

News of the bombing travelled fast around the island. Many Guernsey people phoned their family and friends who had already been evacuated to tell them what was going on and they were even more terrified of what would happen next. Many, who at first had decided to stay, changed their minds and now wanted to evacuate. However, it was too late. No more boats were coming to take them to England. Guernsey was now cut off from the rest of the world and all the islanders could do was wait.

*German planes roared overhead,*
*bombing St Peter Port harbour*
*and the surrounding area.*

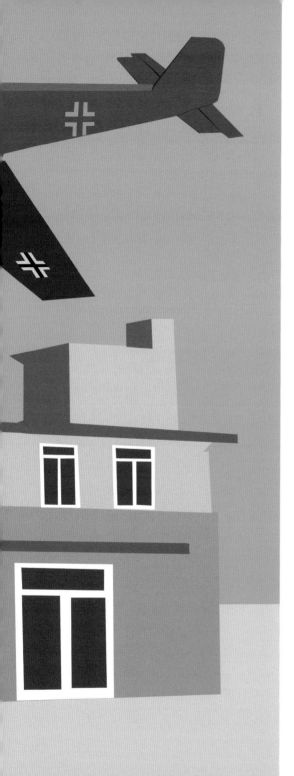

# THE GERMANS ARRIVE

**The islanders did not have to wait long before their final days of freedom were over.**

Two days after the bombings, on Sunday 30th June 1940, a plane from the Luftwaffe flew over the airport. It reported back that the island was defenceless – not a single gun or soldier in sight. The plane was told to land at the empty airport and soon large planes full of soldiers arrived. The first Germans had landed in Guernsey and their flag, the Swastika, was raised at all of the island's important buildings.

The German Occupation of Guernsey had begun.

The Germans swiftly took charge and set up headquarters at The Channel Islands Hotel on Glategny Esplanade in St Peter Port. Occupying the Channel Islands was of great value to the Germans. They had conquered their first British territory. This was a sign to the German people that the war was going well.

*German planes landed at Guernsey's airport and they took control of the island.*

13

# RULES AND REGULATIONS

**The following morning on Monday 1st July, the Guernsey people woke up to a headline on the front of the newspapers that they had been dreading to see – 'Orders of the Commandant of the German Forces in Occupation of the Island of Guernsey'.**

These orders set out strict rules which the locals had to obey. Now nearly every part of island life was heavily restricted and controlled.

One of the rules was a curfew. This meant that between 11pm and 6am the locals were not permitted to leave their homes. The Germans also threatened to bomb the town if anyone caused trouble, the private use of cars was banned and supporting the British was forbidden.

As the occupation continued the Germans issued new rules and life for the local people changed even more. One of the rules introduced in 1941 meant that identity cards with photographs had to be carried at all times. Another stated that locals would have to take in lodgers if commanded to. This meant that some people were now forced to live with Germans in their own homes.

The locals had no choice but to obey these rules or face arrest and imprisonment and so they nervously got used to a new way of life.

**DID YOU KNOW?**

**One strange rule was that cyclists could only ride in single file and the police could fine you if you were caught riding alongside someone else!**

*The rules that were issued by the Germans when they first arrived in Guernsey.*

# ORDERS OF THE COMMANDANT OF THE GERMAN FORCES IN OCCUPATION OF THE ISLAND OF GUERNSEY

(1)- ALL INHABITANTS MUST BE INDOORS BY 11 P.M. AND MUST NOT LEAVE THEIR HOMES BEFORE 6 A.M.

(2)- WE WILL RESPECT THE POPULATION IN GUERNSEY; BUT SHOULD ANYONE ATTEMPT TO CAUSE THE LEAST TROUBLE, SERIOUS MEASURES WILL BE TAKEN AND THE TOWN WILL BE BOMBED.

(3)- ALL ORDERS GIVEN BY THE MILITARY AUTHORITY ARE TO BE STRICTLY OBEYED.

(4)- ALL SPIRITS MUST BE LOCKED UP IMMEDIATELY, AND NO SPIRITS MAY BE SUPPLIED, OBTAINED OR CONSUMED HENCEFORTH. THIS PROHIBITION DOES NOT APPLY TO STOCKS IN PRIVATE HOUSES.

(5)- NO PERSON SHALL ENTER THE AERODROME AT LA VILLIAZE

(6)- ALL RIFLES, AIRGUNS, PISTOLS, REVOLVERS,DAGGERS, SPORTING GUNS AND ALL OTHER WEAPONS WHATSOEVER, EXCEPT SOUVENIRS, MUST TOGETHER WITH ALL AMMUNITION, BE DELIVERED AT THE ROYAL HOTEL BY 12 NOON TODAY, JULY 1.

(7)- ALL BRITISH SOLDIERS AIRMEN AND SOLDIERS ON LEAVE IN THE ISLAND MUST REPORT AT THE POLICE STATION AT 9 A.M. TODAY, AND THEN MUST REPORT AT THE ROYAL HOTEL.

(8)- NO BOAT OR VESSEL OF ANY DESCRIPTION, INCLUDING ANY FISHING BOAT, SHALL LEAVE THE HARBOUR OR ANY OTHER PLACE WHERE THE SAME IS MOORED, WITHOUT AN ORDER FROM THE MILITARY AUTHORITY. TO BE OBTAINED AT THE ROYAL HOTEL. ALL BOATS ARRIVING FROM JERSEY, FROM SARK OR FROM HERM, OR ELSEWHERE, MUST REMAIN IN HARBOUR UNTIL PERMITTED BY THE MILITARY TO LEAVE.

THE CREWS WILL REMAIN ON BOARD. THE MASTER WILL REPORT TO THE HARBOURMASTER, ST PETER PORT, AND WILL OBEY HIS INSTRUCTIONS.

(9)- THE SALE OF MOTOR SPIRIT IS PROHIBITED, EXCEPT FOR USE ON ESSENTIAL SERVICES, SUCH AS DOCTORS' VEHICLES, THE DELIVERY OF FOODSTUFFS, AND SANITARY SERVICES WHERE SUCH VEHICLES ARE IN POSSESSION OF A PERMIT FROM THE MILITARY AUTHORITY TO OBTAIN SUPPLIES.

THESE VEHICLES MUST BE BROUGHT TO THE ROYAL HOTEL BY 12 NOON TODAY TO RECEIVE THE NECESSARY PERMISSION.

THE USE OF CARS FOR PRIVATE PURPOSES IS FORBIDDEN.

(10)- THE BLACK-OUT REGULATIONS ALREADY IN FORCE MUST BE OBSERVED AS BEFORE.

(11)- BANKS AND SHOPS WILL BE OPEN AS USUAL.

(Signed) THE GERMAN COMMANDANT OF THE ISLAND OF GUERNSEY
JULY 1, 1940

# A NEW NORMAL

**Life was very different now. People were separated from their families, strict rules were in place and the island was under enemy control. The first few weeks of the occupation were a strange and difficult time for the local people.**

Despite everything, they went about their business as before but had to consider the new rules and ever-present Germans watching them. Gradually the locals adapted to doing things differently but it wasn't long before these rules, and shortages of food and fuel, started to make life more difficult.

Just before the Germans arrived the States of Deliberation, Guernsey's government, set up a Controlling Committee that would make day-to-day decisions during the occupation. A man called Ambrose Sherwill, who was serving as His Majesty's Attorney General, was elected as President of the Controlling Committee. He was responsible for overseeing the island's affairs and was the direct local contact to the Commandant, the German commanding officer. Ambrose Sherwill served as President until the end of 1940 and the position was then taken over by Jurat John Leale.

> ### JUST IMAGINE...
> **you are keeping an occupation diary. What would you have written about your new life under German rule?**

*Getting used to the new rules was difficult – some people stayed out after the curfew and were nearly caught by the Germans.*

# BACK TO SCHOOL

**Two weeks after the occupation began, Guernsey's schools reopened. Most teachers had evacuated with the children, so there were only a few left to educate approximately 1,050 pupils who had stayed behind. Those who had retired or left to have their own families returned to work during the war to help make up the shortfall of teachers but lessons often had to be taught by untrained teachers such as clergymen and volunteers.**

It was not just the lack of teachers that created challenges. Many of the school buildings had been requisitioned by the Germans so new classrooms had to be found. The schools that did keep their own buildings were not without problems. From early on and throughout the occupation there were shortages of coal and other fuels used for heating. During the bitter winter months, the buildings were extremely cold and this made it difficult for the children to be taught in them.

At the start of the occupation, all children attended their nearest school, including those who were of secondary age so at first there was a large age range of pupils until the Occupation Intermediate School opened for the older children. The war also changed what school children learnt and, at the start of 1943, it became compulsory for them to learn German. The local population and the teachers didn't like this at all. However, they had no choice and so the children were taught German every week.

**WHAT DO YOU THINK...**

**it was like being at school during the occupation?**

**How would you have felt?**

*The Vale School building was used by the Germans so the children had to be taught in the church next door.*

# THE SPIES ARRIVE

**Even though Guernsey had been left undefended, the British authorities still had concern for what was happening on the island and at the beginning of the occupation, they launched some spying missions. Under the cover of darkness, on the 4th September 1940, two former local men, who were now serving British commandos, landed on Petit Port beach in St Martin's on the south coast. Second Lieutenants Hubert Nicolle and James Symes had been chosen by the British for the mission as they had contacts in Guernsey. Nicolle had previously been sent to Guernsey on a mission in July 1940 and had gathered valuable intelligence.**

They had a long and dangerous climb up the steep cliff-face and from there had to make their way to the homes of family and friends without being caught by the Germans. Their orders were to stay on the island for three days gathering intelligence to take back to England and then a boat would be sent to collect them. However, there was a problem. On the night they were due to be picked up the boat didn't arrive. Nicolle and Symes were trapped. This was a disaster. If they were caught as spies they would have been shot and all the people who had helped them would have been in grave trouble.

The President of the Controlling Committee, Ambrose Sherwill, devised a plan. He knew they were on the island and he and his whole committee would have been in serious danger if they were caught. He managed to gather two old Guernsey Militia uniforms for them and doctored them to look like British ones. Their cover story was that they were military personnel who had been trapped in the island when the occupation began, had missed the chance to evacuate and had not given themselves up yet.

The Germans discovered that some British soldiers were hiding on the island. They agreed that there would be an opportunity in early October 1940 for any remaining servicemen to give themselves up and there would be no punishment for those who had helped them. Symes and Nicolle handed themselves over but the Germans didn't stand by their agreement. The British commandos, their family members and other helpers were arrested and deported to France.

As a punishment, the German authorities confiscated everyone's radios. Now the Guernsey people were even more isolated as they could not hear what was happening elsewhere. They were returned in December of that year, the same month that most of the deported family members and helpers of the two men were released from prison in France.

*The spies landed by boat and had to run from the sea and up the beach to the cliffs whilst watching out for any Germans.*

# DEFENDING THE ISLAND

**Occupied rule brought lots of changes to Guernsey's landscape. In October 1941, an order came from Hilter to fortify the Channel Islands to become part of the Atlantic Wall. This was a vast series of fortifications built along the coast of the continent and the Channel Islands as protection in case the Allies tried to attack. Every coastal or important area of Guernsey and the other islands were defended by giant concrete towers, bunkers and gun emplacements and they became one of the most heavily-fortified areas in Europe.**

Over the past centuries, there have been many invaders that have threatened Guernsey and, as a result, the island had lots of fortifications already in place, especially around the coast. These were greatly extended and modernised by the Germans. Many of the defences that remain today are a combination of the old ones and the German ones.

As well as bunkers and gun emplacements, the Germans also installed other defences to protect the island from any attempted attacks. They laid mines in many areas, particularly around the coast. This kept people away from the beaches and cliff paths and would have been hazardous to anyone who had tried to land by sea. Along large flat stretches of L'Ancresse Common they put up poles with wires running across which would have made it impossible for parachutists and paragliders to land. In St Peter Port, explosives were placed under the harbour jetties so they could be blown up if anyone tried to invade the town from the sea.

## DID YOU KNOW?

The largest defence in the Channel Islands was Batterie Mirus.

It is made up of 4 structures that each had a giant gun position.

*Lots of concrete towers and bunkers were built looking out to sea ready to defend Guernsey's coast.*

# BUILDING A FORTRESS

**Even though the Germans ordered the building of the fortifications they didn't carry out the work themselves. This was done by a group of people brought over under Organisation Todt, a construction and engineering organisation set up by the Nazis. A large number of people who were carrying out the work of Organisation Todt were slave workers and forced labourers brought to the Channel Islands to construct fortifications.**

Although occupied life was tough for the locals, for the many thousands of workers it was much, much worse. They were made to work extremely hard for many hours a day with tiny rations of food and poor clothing and footwear which made their jobs much harder. Beatings from the Germans were common and due to the terrible conditions, some of these workers died whilst in Guernsey.

The local people were sympathetic towards these workers and some even tried to help by secretly giving them food. They had to be extremely careful when helping the workers though, as they were forbidden to do so. If they had been caught they could have been severely punished.

**DID YOU KNOW?**

**Many of the workers didn't have proper clothing or shoes.**

**They had to find rags or old sacks to wear.**

*The labourers had to work extremely hard moving heavy equipment and materials.*

# THE GERMAN RAILWAY

**The fortifications were built of reinforced concrete and metal, making them extremely strong and able to withstand a significant attack. To make concrete, sand and stones were used from all over the island. Sand was taken from the northern beaches and the common. Rocks and pebbles were also collected from Guernsey's beaches but the majority of the stone was taken from the quarries that had been in use before the war. Due to their size and weight, these materials were particularly hard to transport around the island.**

By the end of 1941 fortifications were being built all over Guernsey. There was limited transport on the island to carry the equipment and materials to where they were needed. This led to the construction of the German Light Railway which ran around the north, east and west coasts.

The railway carried granite from the quarries to the stone yards at the Bridge where it was crushed into stone chips. From there, the railway carried it around the island for use in the construction of bunkers and towers.

*The railway ran across most of the island to transport building materials.*

26

# TRANSPORT TROUBLES

**Transport was an issue for the locals too. As soon as the occupation began restrictions were placed on civilian transport. The use of private cars was banned. Many of them were requisitioned and then shipped off to the continent or used by the Germans on the island. Some professions required vehicles to carry out their work, such as doctors and the emergency services so they were issued with permits and allocated vehicles.**

From early on in the occupation, fuel shortages were common. This meant that the Germans soon put even more restrictions on transport and many of the motorised vehicles that remained were converted to run on gas instead.

Immediately after the restrictions were announced, bicycles became highly sought after and it was not long until all of the shops had sold out of their entire supply and they had no new stock for the rest of the occupation. As bicycles were the main way to travel around they got a lot of use, which meant that many soon became damaged or worn out, especially the tyres. One of the bicycle shops on the island was called Green's Cycle Shop and they would also do repairs. With no new supplies with which to fix the bicycles, they and the locals became very inventive, using materials such as rubber hoses from the garden for their tyres instead.

**DID YOU KNOW?**

**Cars were hidden away in lots of strange places – some were even buried in haystacks!**

*Green's cycle shop on Smith Street repaired bicycles throughout the war.*

# A LITTLE TIME FOR ENTERTAINMENT

**Although life was difficult, it was not all doom and gloom. The Germans still allowed forms of entertainment with certain rules and conditions. One of the most enjoyable pastimes was to go to the cinema although even during fun times like this, the occupation was never far from sight or mind.**

The cinemas had reminders such as Hitler's photo and German flags outside the entrance, German soldiers had their own areas of seating. Clapping the British forces when they appeared on screen was banned.

Sport continued to be popular too: tennis, football, table tennis and athletics competitions were held regularly.

One of the most favoured forms of entertainment was theatre performances. Local groups would put on plays and concerts which proved popular. The curfew meant it was not possible for those in the rural parishes to come to St Peter Port to see the plays. Often the theatre companies would go out to the churches and halls across the island and perform them there too.

Churches also became popular places for people to meet and to enjoy entertainment and lots of social groups were set up at them throughout the war.

As well as official forms of entertainment there were secret events that took place. House parties were popular and they would often run late into the night, well after the curfew had started. Those at the parties would sometimes stay overnight at the house they were visiting but often they would sneak home well after the curfew had begun. If they heard the familiar sound of Germans approaching they would quickly leap behind the nearest wall or hedge to avoid being spotted and arrested. There were often close encounters with the Germans whilst breaking curfew.

*The Gaumont Cinema on St Julian's Avenue was a popular place for people to go.*

# RADIOS AND RISKS

**One of the best ways for the islanders to keep in touch with what was going on in England and the war effort was through their radios called wireless sets. As the war progressed the Germans used wireless sets as a way of punishing the locals and would threaten them with confiscation if anyone was caught doing anything that was forbidden.**

Radio sets were first confiscated in Autumn 1940 as a reprisal for Hubert Nicolle and James Symes landing on the south coast of Guernsey to spy. They were later returned in time for Christmas in December of that year. Then, in June 1942, the radios were taken once again and their usage was forbidden for the rest of the occupation. The radio sets were rounded up and were meant to be kept safely until the end of the war when they would be returned to their rightful owners. Instead, many of them were used by the German troops and even shipped off-island for use in France, so many people never saw their sets again.

Lots of islanders were not happy about having to hand over their possessions to the Germans and refused to do so. They kept them hidden away at home in a variety of strange places, such as under floorboards or in haystacks, where they were unlikely to be discovered. Those who didn't hide away their radios made or bought crystal sets. These were homemade radios and became popular at the time. The Germans knew that the locals were hiding radios and going against their orders. It was common for the Germans to march into houses unannounced and conduct searches from top to bottom if they suspected the occupants of concealing a wireless set, so it was always essential to be on guard. Those caught with a radio faced arrest, imprisonment and even deportation.

*Islanders would secretly listen to their wireless sets at home before carefully hiding them away.*

# THE GUERNSEY UNDERGROUND NEWS SERVICE

**By mid-1942 Guernsey was completely isolated. Radios had been confiscated and the newspapers were heavily censored by the Germans. The local people had no way of discovering what was really happening elsewhere and, importantly, how the British war effort was progressing. The only news they had access to was what the occupiers were relaying, and this was often heavily biased towards them and their successes.**

Every single thing that was written for the newspapers had to be reviewed by the Germans and anything they didn't agree with was removed or blocked out. Some locals were able to hear the real news stories on their hidden wireless sets and would tune in to the BBC to listen to the British news. Those doing this would spread what they had heard to others who didn't have radios. However, once the news had been retold a few times it had become like a game of Chinese whispers and the stories were not always being recalled accurately.

To be able to get correct information to as wide an audience as possible led to a group of local people undertaking a highly risky venture called the Guernsey Underground News Service or GUNS. This was an alternative secret news source that, for nearly two years, provided the locals with the real news and kept them up to date with the British war effort.

The operation started in 1942. Each night, Henrietta Gillingham and her husband Joseph would take out their secret wireless set to hear the BBC news and would write down the main stories. They would make copies and then pass these on to Henrietta's brother Ernest Legg who would listen to the news the following morning, adding what he had heard to the sheets. Next, they would be passed on to Charles Machon who was working for The Star newspaper. He used his access to materials to print the new sheets and then copies were shared and handed out to reach as many people as possible. Those who had copies of the sheets had to be extremely careful with them. They had to be quietly passed around, watching out for the Germans so they didn't catch a glimpse. If they were caught with them, they and the GUNS members would have been arrested.

In 1943 Henrietta pulled out of the operation when she became pregnant as she was fearful of the risks she was taking. By this time GUNS had two new members, Frank Falla and Cecil

Duquemin, and, together with the original members, they continued to produce the sheets until the night of the 11th February 1944.

On this particular evening, GUNS was betrayed by an informer who had reported the members to the German authorities. They were arrested, interrogated and eventually deported from the island to serve their prison sentences in France and Germany. The conditions in these prisons were awful and of the 5 members deported only 3 returned to Guernsey. Sadly both Joseph Gillingham and Charles Machon died whilst in prison.

After the war and to the present day this brave group of people are still remembered as true heroes of the occupation. They risked their freedom and lives to keep people informed of the real news and gave the local people hope at the darkest times of occupied life.

*Each evening the GUNS members would listen to the news and prepare for the next day's news sheets.*

# WAR ORGANISATION OF THE BRITISH RED CROSS AND ORDER OF ST JOHN

**Expediteur SENDER Absender**

Name .... *Torode* ....................................
Nom
Christian name .... *Julia* ..........................
Vorname
Address .... *Baildon, Yorkshire,* ..........
Adresse .... *England* ..............................

.................................................................

**MESSAGE Mitteilung**

(Not more than 25 words) (25 mots au maximum) (Nicht ober 25 Worte)

*All well. Margaret had nice*
*birthday. Always in our*
*thoughts. Love to all.*
...........................................................
 ..................................

Date Datum ..........................................

**Destinataire ADDRESSEE Empfanger**

Name .... *Torode* .................................
Nom
Christian name .... *John* .......................
Vorname
Address .... *3, Church Lane,* ................
Adresse .... *St Sampson, Guernsey,* .....
.... *Channel Islands* ...........................

Reply overleaf (not more than 25 words)

# LETTERS FROM LOVED ONES

**When the Germans arrived they ceased all contact between England and the Channel Islands. This included all telephone calls and postal services and so when children and other residents evacuated in June 1940 there was no way of contacting them.**

It was a great relief when in early 1941, a local Red Cross bureau was set up to handle the sending, receiving and distribution of letters. One of the founding members of the Red Cross in Guernsey was a local lady called Léonie Trouteaud and throughout the war, she and her colleagues worked tirelessly to process all of the messages coming in and going out under the watchful eyes of the German authorities.

In February 1941 the first batch of 1,900 messages arrived on the island and finally the local people had some idea of how their friends and family over on the mainland were doing. They weren't able to get too much of an update as the messages were limited to very few words. Replies were written on the back of the original message and it could take several months for them to arrive. This wasn't a quick way to communicate but the locals were grateful for the letters after many months of no contact.

When writing a message it was important to be careful about what information was being shared. All of them had to be checked by the Germans before they were sent to ensure no one was giving away secrets about what was happening on the island. Often people would write codes that could only be understood by family members. This made the Germans suspicious of the content so often they would censor messages or demand letters were investigated to ensure that no one was defying their orders.

**JUST IMAGINE...**

You haven't seen your parents for a year.

Write a Red Cross message to them using no more than 25 words.

*The locals were grateful to receive their Red Cross letters from friends and relatives.*

# FORCED TO LEAVE

**One of the darkest periods of the occupation was the deportation of islanders by the German authorities to the continent. Deportations were carried out against those who the German feared may be a threat to their power and security, people from certain religions and backgrounds and also as threats and reprisals against the locals and Allies.**

In April 1942, three Jewish women were deported from Guernsey and sent to Auschwitz concentration camp. The Nazis sent millions of Jewish people and other groups to concentration camps in Europe and huge numbers, including the three women from Guernsey, were murdered.

In September 1942, all non-Guernsey-born men and their families were deported on Hitler's orders. A few months later, in February 1943, further deportations were ordered. Over 1,000 people from Guernsey were taken to the continent and sent to internment camps. The Germans had also deported others including those with a prison record and anyone with a military background. Those convicted of committing crimes were also often sent away from the island to serve their sentences.

For those deported it was terrifying and distressing to be ordered to leave their homes against their will simply because of the place they were born or their religion. They didn't know where they would be taken and when they arrived at the camps they were kept in terrible conditions, with little food and no idea of when they would be free. Due to the conditions, many fell ill and some died whilst there. The remaining islanders had seen friends and family members being taken away and they didn't know who would be next. They were terrified it could be them too.

**DID YOU KNOW?**

Most of the deported Channel Islanders went to three camps in Germany.

Families were sent to Biberach and Wurzach and single men were sent to Laufen.

*The Germans issued orders forcing groups of locals to leave the island.*

Guernsey den 15, September 1942

# NOTICE

By order of higher authorities the following British subjects will be evacuated and transferred to Germany:

a) Persons who have their permanent residence not on the Channel Islands, for instance those who have been caught here by the outbreak of war,

b) all those men not born on the Channel Islands and 16 to 70 years of age who belong to the English people, together with their families.

Detailed instructions will be given by the Feldkommandantur

# DISOBEYING THE GERMANS

**The vast majority of islanders were law-abiding during the occupation but there were always some who were happy to bend or break the rules, although the punishments and reprisals should they be caught doing so were severe.**

Throughout the war, there were various forms of resistance by the islanders against the German authorities and their rules. Painting 'V' for victory signs on houses and buildings was a common form and the Germans eventually adopted their own version of the sign as they could not stop it spreading. Protesting against the German rules or control, hiding away radios or passing on British news or propaganda were also regular forms of resistance that were carried out by locals.

Resistance against the Germans was a highly risky thing to do. Those that committed serious crimes in Guernsey were sent to Jersey to face trial there and then would be issued with their punishment. Sentences were harsh and were often long terms in prison, usually served on the continent. Shorter sentences for minor wrongdoings were normally spent in the Guernsey prison on St James Street in St Peter Port.

The Germans discovered many acts of resistance due to informers. These were local people who would report their fellow islanders in return for preferential treatment from the Germans. Informers were disliked by the other Guernsey people – the islanders were meant to stick together and not betray each other. Some people were deported from the island because of informers, even when the accusations were false. Informers believed that they would be looked upon favourably by the German authorities.

*'V' signs were often painted on walls,*
*houses and buildings.*

# DARING TO ESCAPE

**Life under occupied rule was very difficult. Lots of parents were left without their children, families were separated and being apart began to take its toll quickly. Lots of men were left alone on Guernsey without their wives and children after the evacuations. These situations and the conditions on the island led some locals to attempt the risky and illegal feat of escaping in fishing boats.**

In September 1940, a group of islanders managed to escape from Bordeaux Harbour under the cover of darkness. They rowed out for half a mile so that no one would hear the motor on the boat and then made their way across the English Channel. Not long into the journey, a flare was dropped by a German plane flying overhead. Terrified, they lay still at the bottom of the boat until it had burnt out and miraculously they were not seen.

It wasn't long until the Germans discovered that the men had gone. They were furious and announced that all fishing boats were to be brought to St Peter Port harbour. The President of the Controlling Committee, Ambrose Sherwill, issued a notice explaining that the Germans had banned fishing and there would be serious repercussions should anyone try to escape again. The locals were warned that if they left the island, it would be their fellow islanders who would suffer.

In 1943, seven more people escaped: four men and three women. That night there was a bright full moon which illuminated them but they managed to get away from the coast without being spotted. After this, access to the beaches was forbidden and fishing was banned for five weeks. Many people relied on fishing to overcome the shortage of other foods – so this ban made matters worse.

*The boat was prepared for the islanders to escape under the cover of darkness from Bordeaux Harbour.*

# A STRUGGLE TO SURVIVE

**The shortage of food was one of the biggest problems for the Guernsey people during the occupation. Due to the evacuation in 1940, the island had good food supplies when the Germans arrived. There were ample stocks of canned fruit, vegetables and sugar. However many of the Germans who had arrived had come from France where shortages were common. They could not believe their eyes when they saw the food and other goods that were in the shops and they quickly bought up much of it to use and to send back to their families in Germany.**

Before the war, all of Guernsey's imported food came from England. Without the supplies from the mainland, it didn't take long until stocks began to dwindle and shortages became common.

A purchasing commission was set up, headed by Raymond Falla, to buy food for the local population, based in Granville in France. Throughout the war, they worked tirelessly to provide as much food for the island as they could. This was a huge challenge. France did not have many supplies either so buying everything that was needed was not an easy task. By 1942 food and other household items were running out rapidly and supplies were becoming harder to come by. People were longing for items that before the war they had taken for granted.

These shortages led to a small number of local people trying their luck at making money in illegal ways and it wasn't long before a black market emerged on the island. This meant that people who had extra food and other items would illegally sell them for far more than they were worth to make lots of money for themselves. Those caught trading in it faced serious punishments such as prison sentences and large fines. Despite the best efforts of the courts to find and punish those engaging in the black market, it didn't stop it flourishing as people were so desperate to get their hands on scarce foods and luxuries.

When food supplies did arrive there was a rush to get to the shops to buy it before it ran out again. People would queue for hours in town to purchase their rations. Despite supplies arriving, it didn't guarantee that islanders would get the food they needed. Many would queue for hours only to discover that what they had waited so patiently for had sold out.

Food and household items were not the only things running out. Clothing and footwear were in short supply. With no new material arriving to make clothes, there was no choice but to repair what they had. This was a problem for children who were outgrowing their clothes. Blankets would be cut up and made into coats for the winter months. From early on in the occupation fuel supplies began running out. As it became more scarce, it made it difficult for people to prepare meals. This led to communal kitchens being set up in different parishes so that lots of people could cook together, using less fuel.

*People would queue outside shops for hours waiting for their rations.*

The Vega made trips to Guernsey during the occupation and saved the locals from starvation.

# SAVED BY THE VEGA

**On Tuesday 6th June 1944 one of the most important events of the Second World War took place. The Allied forces launched the Normandy Landings, the largest ever seaborne invasion of the French coast, often referred to as 'D-Day'. Allied success in the mission meant the start of the liberation of France from German control and this was a turning point in the eventual overall Allied victory.**

The Guernsey people who had hidden away wireless sets heard all about the D-Day landings and successes on the news. It brought a lot of hope as they thought this meant that the war would soon be over. However little did they know, it would be nearly another year until liberation was to come to the Channel Islands.

Even though D-Day was a boost for the loyal and patriotic Channel Islanders, it brought with it significant problems. Many of the vital food supply routes were cut off. No longer being able to import goods from France meant that Guernsey was using its final stocks of food and these were rapidly running out. Guernsey people were beginning to starve and, as the winter of 1944 approached, the situation was becoming desperate. It was estimated that by the end of January 1945 Guernsey would have used up its entire supply of food and there would be nothing left for the islanders to eat.

An appeal was sent to the Red Cross asking them to urgently bring food and medical supplies to the Channel Islands. On the 27th December 1944, the Red Cross ship the SS Vega arrived into St Peter Port harbour, bringing with it the much-longed-for food parcels and medical supplies. This ship was a delightful sight to the Guernsey people who without it would have undoubtedly starved. The Vega made a further 4 trips back to the island between December 1944 and liberation in May 1945 and is credited with saving the lives of many islanders.

# TERRIBLE TIMES

**Life as a whole was difficult under occupied rule. However, there were some significant events that were more difficult than most. Because of the defences built all over the island, lots of places became dangerous to visit. Accidents occurred involving mines which had been laid around the coast. Although locals were warned to stay away, some tried their luck at finding shortcuts home or to the coast but were seriously injured or killed in explosions.**

Planes were often seen roaring overhead and it was sometimes possible to see or hear fighting taking place in the sky. It was always very sad to see a plane shot down, whichever side it was from. Often the islanders would see the German planes flying overhead in the direction of the mainland. It brought them much sadness to see Britain about to be attacked and of course fear for their families and friends.

One of the most well-known events of the occupation was the sinking of the British ships HMS Charybdis and HMS Limbourne in October 1943. Tragically many sailors on these ships lost their lives and many locals were saddened by this news. Some of those who died were buried at the Foulon Cemetery in St Peter Port with the Germans giving them a respectful military funeral. Locals were allowed to attend and over 5,000 came to pay their respects, laying hundreds of wreaths. This event showed the strength of their loyalty to the British and from then on civilians were restricted from attending military funerals. A ceremony to commemorate this tragedy is still held every year.

The conditions under which the Organisation Todt workers were forced to live were extremely hard for the islanders to witness. They were treated horrendously and had next to no food. It distressed many islanders to see their fellow humans being treated so badly. Because of the lack of food, workers took to sneaking into gardens to steal from greenhouses or stores. At this time pets began to go missing, often stolen by the Germans or workers to eat.

*Many areas of the island were heavily mined and signs were put up like this one saying 'Danger Mines!'.*

THESE GATE POSTS MARK THE
ENTRANCE TO THE FORMER
GERMAN CONCENTRATION CAMP
**"S.S LAGER SYLT"**

SOME 400 PRISONERS DIED HERE
BETWEEN
MARCH 1943 AND JUNE 1944
THIS PLAQUE WAS PLACED BY
EX- PRISONERS AND THEIR
FAMILIES
2008

*The gate posts at the entrance to one of the camps on Alderney, Lager Sylt.*

# ALDERNEY: ALTERED BEYOND RECOGNITION

**Despite all being under the same enemy control the experiences of all the Channel Islands differed greatly. Alderney is the second-largest island in the Bailiwick, lying just 10 miles off the coast of France. When the news of the impending occupation arrived, all but a few of Alderney's residents were evacuated to safety by the Royal Navy.**

They were permitted to take a single suitcase each in which they had to fit all of their most treasured possessions and everything they needed. As the ships sailed away and Alderney faded into the distance, the locals took a last look at the island as they knew it. Little did they know that it would look very different five years later when they returned.

As so many of Alderney's residents had evacuated, much of the food and livestock that would have otherwise gone to waste was rounded up and shipped to Guernsey. The farming land that was left unattended was put to good use. At the start of the occupation, a team of Guernseymen were sent to work in Alderney, using the island to grow crops that could be sent back to feed the islanders. However, this was stopped in 1942 when the Germans found a more sinister use for Alderney.

The island became home to four camps for thousands of men brought over as prisoners and labourers under Organisation Todt. These men, like the ones in Guernsey, were brought over to construct fortifications. In 1941 Hitler issued an order to fortify the Channel Islands, including Alderney. Despite being small, many defensive structures were built here. For the men brought over, there was no escape from the brutal and inhumane treatment and hundreds died whilst there.

Liberation came for Alderney on the 16th May 1945. However, there were no joyous celebrations like there were on Guernsey. The first islanders arrived back in Alderney on the 15th December 1945 which is still known as Homecoming Day. As delighted as they were to be home again this was not the time for celebration. They were faced with an unimaginable scale of change and destruction. The landscape had been altered completely with camps built over the open land and the majority of the private homes having been lived in by the Germans. Their island home was very different from the place they once knew.

# SARK: SMALL BUT MIGHTY

**When the Germans first set foot on Sark, the third largest island in the Bailiwick, they were greeted by its leader, the Dame of Sark, Sibyl Hathaway. She had the benefit of speaking fluent German and could communicate with the occupiers in their own language and this, alongside her forceful manner, gained her respect from the enemy authorities.**

The Dame had encouraged the people of Sark to stay and to try to carry on with their daily lives. Just over 450 remained. Many of the islanders worked as fishermen and they were allowed to continue sending two boats to Guernsey each week to sell their catch. During the first summers of the occupation, the Germans even allowed people from Guernsey to go on holiday to Sark.

Due to Dame Sibyl, the relations between the Sarkees and the Germans started out on fairly good terms. However, this all changed after a failed raid called Operation Basalt led by the British in October 1942. A group of British Commandos had tried to raid the island to capture the Germans. When they landed they were helped by a local lady who gave them information. The raid went wrong and the British had to retreat with haste, with three German soldiers killed in the process. The Germans were furious at what had happened. They mined the entire coastline, making much of the island dangerous and inaccessible. They also brought over more troops bringing the total number to 500, meaning there were more Germans than Sarkees on the island.

Just like in Guernsey, the people of Sark had to live under the same set of strict rules. They were also affected by deportations, with non-locally born people being sent to camps on the continent. This included Dame Sibyl's husband Robert Hathaway who was ordered to leave as he was American. Food shortages badly affected Sark too. The locals tried to grow and fish as much as they could but, towards the end of the war, they relied on the parcels sent by the Red Cross.

The end of the occupation for Sark came on the 10th May 1945. The locals had listened to Winston Churchill's speech on the 8th May and knew that they were free. Two days later the British arrived on Sark to accept the German surrender. Dame Sibyl Hathaway was in charge once again and soon her husband and the other deportees were returned home.

Dame Sibyl Hathaway greeted the Germans
at her home, La Seigneurie.

# FREEDOM, FINALLY

**After D-Day islanders had been hoping that the war would soon be over. Towards the end of 1944, the British had been dropping leaflets to try to persuade the Germans to surrender. All of this gave hope to the Guernsey people that the end of the war was on its way and they would once again be free. They waited eagerly to hear any updates. The news was being spread by those who still had access to radios and by the spring of 1945 rumours were circulating that the war was going to end very soon.**

The news of freedom that the islanders had waited five long years to hear came on Tuesday 8th May 1945. The Guernsey people crowded into each other's homes where the once-concealed wireless sets were brought out from their hiding places. They gathered around and listened to a speech from the Prime Minister of the United Kingdom, Winston Churchill, who announced that the war was over and declared that: "Our dear Channel Islands are also to be freed today". The islanders were jubilant, the war was over and they were free from German rule. The houses were covered with Union Jacks and bunting to mark the momentous day.

The Germans signed the official surrender documents the next day, Wednesday 9th May. It was a beautiful, sunny day and anyone who could make the trip into town did so. The view was glorious. Waiting in the Little Russel were the Allied ships that had arrived to free the island. The seafront was packed tightly with people all hoping to catch a glimpse of the liberating soldiers from Task Force 135 as they came ashore. Five years of heartbreak and hardship was over and normal life could soon resume. Those who had evacuated could come home and families could reunite.

They were once again free, reunited with Britain where they belonged.

*The locals covered their houses with Union Jacks and bunting to celebrate the liberation.*

# RETURNING AND REUNITING

**Even though the war was over, the challenges did not end there for the locals. Guernsey and the other Channel Islands were left with a huge clean-up operation. The island had to be made safe once again and much of what the Germans had left behind had to be cleared. In July 1945, the first evacuees returned to Guernsey.**

The returning evacuees had a shock when they saw the island again. Many areas were barely recognisable. The once pretty coastline was now crowded with ugly concrete structures and littered with mines, making the whole area out of bounds. Houses had been ransacked by the Germans who had taken everything. Others returned to find their houses had been lived in by the Germans or Organisation Todt workers and were so badly kept they were not even habitable. Even worse, some houses had been destroyed altogether to make way for fortifications or the railway.

Over five years children had grown up and some people didn't even recognise their family members when they got off the boats. Despite the time that had lapsed and the things that had changed, it was wonderful to be reunited.

Guernsey still celebrates the anniversary of liberation on the 9th May each year. It is an important day to remember the people who lived and died during the occupation and to be grateful for the freedom that the Bailiwick of Guernsey has now.

*The locals were delighted to come back and reunite with their family and friends.*

# MAIN LOCATIONS

There are lots of locations connected to the occupation in Guernsey.

This map shows where some of the main events occurred and where the important places are or would have been at the time.

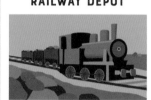

RAILWAY DEPOT

FORT SAUMAREZ

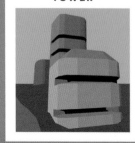

OBSERVATION TOWER

GUERNSEY AIRPORT

## VALE SCHOOL

## BORDEAUX HARBOUR

## GAUMONT CINEMA

## ST PETER PORT HARBOUR

## ARRIVAL OF SS VEGA

## PETIT PORT

# MAIN EVENTS

## 1939

| | |
|---|---|
| **1st September** | The Second World War begins |

## 1940

| | |
|---|---|
| **14th June** | Paris falls to German control |
| **19th June** | The instructions for evacuations are given |
| **20th June** | The first evacuation of schoolchildren from Guernsey |
| **23rd June** | Alderney residents evacuated by the Royal Navy |
| **27th June** | The Luftwaffe is seen flying over Guernsey |
| **28th June** | German bombings of St Peter Port Harbour |
| **30th June** | The German Occupation begins |
| **1st July** | The first German orders are announced |
| **2nd July** | The Germans arrive in Alderney |
| **3rd July** | The Germans arrive in Sark |
| **15th July** | Guernsey's schools reopen |
| **4th September** | British spies Hubert Nicolle and James Symes land on the south coast |
| **September** | Escape from Bordeaux Harbour |

## 1941

| | |
|---|---|
| **February** | The first Red Cross messages arrive in Guernsey |
| **October** | Order issued from Hitler to fortify the Channel Islands |

## 1942

| | |
|---|---|
| **April** | Three Jewish women are deported |
| **May** | GUNS formed |
| **June** | Radios are confiscated until the end of the war |
| **26th-27th Sept.** | English-born men and their families are deported |
| **3rd-4th October** | Operation Basalt carried out in Sark |

## 1943

| | |
|---|---|
| **13th February** | Further deportations are carried out following Operation Basalt |
| **14th August** | Another group of islanders escape from Bordeaux |
| **23rd October** | The sinking of HMS Charybdis and HMS Limbourne |

## 1944

| | |
|---|---|
| **11th February** | The GUNS members are betrayed and arrested |
| **6th June** | The Normandy Landings, also known as D-Day |
| **27th December** | The Vega arrives into St Peter Port Harbour |

## 1945

| | |
|---|---|
| **8th May** | The news of liberation breaks |
| **9th May** | Liberation of Guernsey |
| **10th May** | Liberation of Sark |
| **16th May** | Liberation of Alderney |
| **July** | The first islanders return home to Guernsey. |
| **15th December** | Homecoming Day in Alderney |

# GLOSSARY

**Allied Powers**  Britain, France, the Soviet Union, the United States and other nations who all combined to fight against the Axis powers.

**Attorney General**  Guernsey's most senior lawyer who represents the Crown in legal cases.

**Axis Powers**  Germany, Italy, Japan and other nations who all combined to fight against the Allied powers.

**Bailiwick of Guernsey**  A group of islands made up of Guernsey, Alderney, Sark and Herm and the smaller islands of Jethou and Brecqhou.

**Biased**  Being unfairly for or against something.

**Bureau**  An office, organisation or department who is responsible for carrying out different processes or business.

**Censored**  Examining newspaper reports, news broadcasts or other forms of information being shared with the public and removing any parts deemed unacceptable.

**Commandant**  The officer in charge of the German Forces in Guernsey and the other Channel Islands.

**Confiscated**  When something is taken away or seized by a figure of authority.

**Controlling Committee**  The emergency committee set up to run the island when the Germans occupied.

**Crystal Sets**  A simple form of radio with a crystal touching a metal wire and no loudspeaker meaning headphones were needed. During the occupation these were often home-made and referred to as the 'cat's whiskers'.

**Curfew**  A restriction on people's movements requiring them to stay indoors between certain times.

**Demilitarisation**  The removal or reduction of armed forces from a particular place or country.

| | |
|---|---|
| **Deportations** | The process of removing or expelling someone from a country or place. |
| **Evacuation** | When people are removed from or leave a dangerous place. |
| **Fortify** | To defend somewhere with structures or manpower to protect against an attack. |
| **Guernsey Militia** | A group of military volunteers who defended the island against any threats or invaders. |
| **Informer** | A person who reported other islanders' wrong-doings to the German authorities, often for financial gain or special treatment. |
| **Intelligence** | Collection and processing of information for military or political use. |
| **Liberation** | The act of setting a person or place free from enemy imprisonment or control, in Guernsey's case this was the 9th May 1945. |
| **Little Russel** | The stretch of water between Guernsey and Herm. |
| **Luftwaffe** | The German air force during the Second World War. |
| **Mine** | An explosive device usually placed underground or underwater to defend areas of land or deter from invasion. |
| **Nazi Party** | A political party that was active in Germany between 1920 and 1945. |
| **Organisation Todt** | An engineering firm in Nazi Germany that was responsible for building many fortifications and other stuctures around Europe. |
| **Propaganda** | Biased or misleading information used to promote or portray a particular opinion or political view. |
| **Purchasing committee** | The organisation set up to purchase food to feed the islanders during the occupation. |

**Red Cross**      An organisation that helps those across the world in need or crisis due to conflicts, war and natural disasters.

**Reprisal**      To punish a person or a group of people in retaliation or revenge for something.

**Requisition**      An official order claiming the use of property or materials.

**Resistance**      Organised groups who fight against or stand up to an occupying enemy.

**Royal Court**      Guernsey's highest court that applies the laws of the island and deals with criminal and civil matters.

**Swastika**      The emblem of the Nazi Party used on flags, documents and other places.

**States of Deliberation**      The government of Guernsey.

**V signs**      A sign drawn on buildings, signs and other public places to show support for Allied victory. The Germans could not remove all the signs so adopted their own version instead.

**Wireless Sets**      The name originally used for a radio set.